EXPLORING DINOSAURS & PREHISTORIC CREATURES

ARCHAEOPTERYX

By Susan H. Gray

THE CHILD'S WORLD®
CHANHASSEN, MINNESOTA

The
**Child's
World**®

Published in the United States of America by The Child's World®
PO Box 326, Chanhassen, MN 55317-0326
800-599-READ
www.childsworld.com

Content Adviser:
Brian Huber, PhD,
Curator, Department
of Paleobiology,
Smithsonian
National Museum
of Natural History,
Washington DC

Photo Credits: Sally A. Morgan, Ecoscene/Corbis: 5; Danny Lehman/Corbis: 13; Terry W. Eggers/Corbis: 17; Jonathan Blair/Corbis: 19, 20, 24; Mike Fredericks: 8; the Natural History Museum, London: 4, 6, 11; Lizzie Harper/SPL/Photo Researchers, Inc.: 7; Tom & Pat Leeson/Photo Researchers, Inc.: 9; Chris Butler/SPL/Photo Researchers, Inc.: 12; Roger Harris/SPL/Photo Researchers, Inc.: 14, 23; Pascal Goetgheluck/SPL/Photo Researchers, Inc.: 15; Francois Gohier/Photo Researchers, Inc.: 18; Photo Researchers, Inc.: 26; Gregory G. Dimijian/Photo Researchers, Inc.: 27; Ken Lucas/Visuals Unlimited: 21.

The Child's World®: Mary Berendes, Publishing Director

Editorial Directions, Inc.: E. Russell Primm, Editorial Director; Pam Rosenberg, Line Editor; Katie Marsico, Associate Editor; Matthew Messbarger, Editorial Assistant; Susan Hindman, Copy Editor; Melissa McDaniel, Proofreader; Tim Griffin/IndexServ, Indexer; Olivia Nellums, Fact Checker; Dawn Friedman, Photo Researcher; Linda S. Koutris, Photo Selector

Original cover art by Todd Marshall

The Design Lab: Kathleen Petelinsek, Design; Kari Thornborough, Page Production

Library of Congress Cataloging-in-Publication Data
Gray, Susan Heinrichs.
  Archaeopteryx / by Susan H. Gray.
    p. cm. — (Exploring dinosaurs & prehistoric creatures)
  Includes index.
  ISBN 1-59296-364-1 (lib. bound : alk. paper)
  1. Archaeopteryx—Juvenile literature. I. Title.
  QE872.A8G73 2005
  568'.22—dc22   2004018059

TABLE OF CONTENTS

CHAPTER ONE

A Fatal Mistake

Archaeopteryx (AR-kee-OP-ter-ix) swerved and dipped in the air. She was determined to catch a dragonfly that had just zipped by. The dragonfly made a quick turn to the left, but *Archaeopteryx* wasn't fast enough. She plunged, headfirst, right into the **lagoon.**

The bird tried to squawk, but instead, she gulped a mouthful of water. The water was incredibly salty. It stung her throat. It burned her lungs. It made her feel sick to her stomach.

Archaeopteryx *had an average wingspan of 1.5 feet (0.5 meters).*

Scientists found this Archaeopteryx *skeleton in Germany.*

Archaeopteryx thrashed about, trying to lift herself from the pool,

but it did no good. She sucked in more and more of the awful water.

Soon, exhausted and sickened, she sank to the bottom.

Time passed, and her body became **embedded** in the soft

mud of the lagoon's floor. Fine grains of dirt in the water settled over

the bird, covering her like a blanket. *Archaeopteryx* lay in silence for

millions of years while the layers piled higher and higher.

CHAPTER TWO

WHAT WAS ARCHAEOPTERYX?

Archaeopteryx was a bird that lived about 150 million years ago. In fact, it is the earliest bird known. Its name is taken from Greek words that mean "**ancient** wing." An *Archaeopteryx* adult was about the size of a crow and weighed about 1 pound (454 grams).

Scientists consider Archaeopteryx *the earliest known bird, but it also had several reptilelike qualities.*

Archaeopteryx used its clawed fingers and sharp teeth to hunt insects and small lizards.

Archaeopteryx had a long neck and a very long tail. It had a large brain and big eyes. Unlike birds of today, its beak was lined with many teeth.

The bird's wings were quite unusual. The hand bones of modern birds are covered with skin and feathers. *Archaeopteryx* had hand

Although Archaeopteryx *had feathered wings, scientists don't believe it flew very well.*

bones that were out in the open. Three long, clawed fingers extended from the front edge of each wing. The claws were curved and may have helped the bird catch **prey** and climb trees.

Archaeopteryx also had long legs and might have walked more than it flew. Its feet were built like those of many modern birds. Three toes pointed forward and one toe pointed backward. Toes arranged in this way help birds perch on tree limbs. Like its fingers, the toes of *Archaeopteryx* also ended in claws.

CHAPTER THREE

THE DINOSAUR-BIRD

Although *Archaeopteryx* was a bird, it had many things in common with the dinosaurs. For instance, *Archaeopteryx* had a full set of teeth. Modern birds are not armed with teeth, but many dinosaurs were.

Flying birds have strong muscles in their chests. These flight muscles are attached to the

Both *Archaeopteryx* and this modern-day bald eagle share certain characteristics. The eagle, however, has strong chest muscles and no teeth.

breastbone or sternum, which has a large, flat outgrowth known as a keel. In animals that don't fly, the sternum is small and there is no keel. The feathered wings of *Archaeopteryx* were birdlike, but its little sternum was more like that of a small dinosaur.

Most birds have collar bones that fuse together in the center. We sometimes call these bones the wishbone. Very few dinosaurs had a wishbone, but it was certainly present in *Archaeopteryx*.

Many dinosaurs had a set of slender bones embedded in the flesh of their bellies. These bones are called belly ribs or gastralia (gas-TRAY-lee-uh). In large dinosaurs, such as *Allosaurus* (AL-oh-SAWR-us), gastralia might have protected the animal's organs or added strength to the belly wall. *Archaeopteryx* also had gastralia, but no one knows why. Modern birds have no such structures.

The tail of *Archaeopteryx* was long—almost as long as the rest

of the body. A series of bones ran out to the tip of the tail, as it

did in the dinosaurs. These bones were covered with flesh from

which feathers grew. In modern birds, the tailbone is very short,

and the feathers themselves give the tail its length. Even in birds

such as peacocks, the tailbone is not long at all.

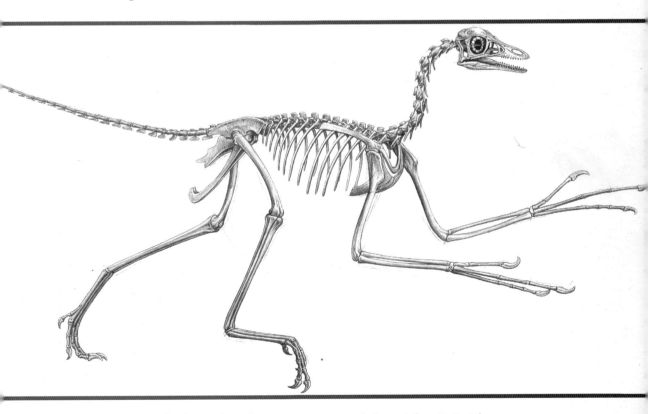

From beak to tail, Archaeopteryx *measured about 1 foot (0.3m) long.*

Like Archaeopteryx, Allosaurus *(shown here) had gastralia.*
Both creatures lived during the same time period.

It seems that *Archaeopteryx* was very birdlike but also very similar

to the dinosaurs. Because it had so many things in common with

the dinosaurs, scientists believe that dinosaurs were the **ancestors**

of birds.

WHERE ARE ALL THE BIRD FOSSILS?

Scientists have discovered thousands of dinosaur fossils. However, bird fossils are fairly rare. Why are they so hard to find?

There are several reasons why bird fossils are not that common. Bird skeletons have hollow bones and are very lightweight. Such skeletons are easily crushed, can fall apart quickly, or can be eaten by other animals. Also, because birds are such small creatures, they leave only small skeletons behind. It's easy for fossil hunters to miss them.

Ancient animals left more than their bones behind. Some left other signs such as footprints (below) and tooth marks. Big 3-ton dinosaurs would have left lots of footprints behind in muddy areas. In many cases, scientists have found these footprints and have been able to tell the kinds of dinosaur that left them. Birds, however, barely make footprints at all. Therefore, scientists do not find them very often.

Big meat eaters such as *Tyrannosaurus* (tuh-RAN-uh-SAWR-us) *rex* (left) left another sign of their presence. They left tooth marks in the bones of their prey. Scientists have discovered bite marks in the bones of certain dinosaurs that lived at the same time as *T. rex*. The bite marks exactly match the big, fierce teeth of *T. rex*. But what kind of tooth marks would birds leave behind? None. Most birds didn't have teeth. Those that did, such as *Archaeopteryx,* ate small animals and insects. If they got the chance to leave tooth marks on something, they probably swallowed it!

CHAPTER FOUR

WHAT DID ARCHAEOPTERYX DO ALL DAY?

*A*rchaeopteryx probably spent most of its day chasing insects, eating them, and sleeping. It swooped through the air to catch flying insects, and it trotted along the ground to catch running ones. Even the biggest dragonflies and cockroaches were easily crunched up in its toothy jaws.

This dragonfly would have made a tasty treat for a hungry Archaeopteryx. *In prehistoric times, dragonflies had a wingspan of up to 30 inches (76 centimeters).*

On hot days, the bird may have acted much like its modern

relatives do, splashing in puddles and fanning its wings to cool off.

During cold nights, it probably hunkered down, letting its feathers

insulate its body.

At some time during the year, *Archaeopteryx* males courted females.

Of course, no one knows how they did this, but they probably used

some sort of **display.** Modern birds do this all the time. Males dance,

strut, sing, and show off their handsome feathers to attract females.

If *Archaeopteryx* had bright colors, perhaps the males spread their wings

to show off. Maybe they waved their magnificent tails. Perhaps they

pranced around with ruffled feathers to win over the females.

Like dinosaurs and birds, *Archaeopteryx* would have laid eggs. But

scientists don't know how many eggs it laid at a time or how the baby

birds were treated by their parents. No *Archaeopteryx* eggs or nests have

A brightly colored peacock displays his tail feathers to attract a mate.

been found, so no one knows how they tended their young. It is

possible that the birds nested on the ground. Some birds of today,

such as wild turkeys and meadowlarks, build ground nests.

It is also possible that *Archaeopteryx* nested in trees. One modern-day bird that nests in trees near water is the hoatzin (waht-SEEN) of South America. The young have claws on their wings, just as *Archaeopteryx* did. In times of danger, baby hoatzins leap from the nest to the water below. When it's safe again, they swim to shore and climb back up to the nest using their feet and wing claws. Perhaps *Archaeopteryx* babies did this, too, but we will probably never know.

A mother hoatzin feeds her chicks. Hoatzins make their homes in Amazon rain forests.

GERMANY'S TREASURES

Long ago, a place in southern Germany became the perfect fossil grave-yard. Now known as the Solnhofen (SO-len-HO-fen) Limestone, it is famous for its many fine fossils. What happened so long ago that made this such a treasure trove of fossils today?

About 150 million years ago, much of Germany was covered with warm, shallow waters. In these warm seas, coral reefs grew up from the ocean floor. As the reefs grew taller, they divided the sea into many separate pools, or lagoons. Because the reefs protected the lagoons from waves, these pools were very calm. Over time, the water in the pools became quite salty and low in oxygen. Plants and animals that floated or fell into these lagoons did not live long. They died, sank to the bottom, and were covered with fine silt. No other creatures ate them, because nothing else could live in the salty, oxygen-poor water.

Millions of years passed. More and more animals sank to the bottom, and more and more silt covered them up. Finally, the waters drew back and dry land appeared. By then, all sorts of animals had been buried inside layers of fine-grained rock.

Years ago, people in Germany began finding those animals. They found beautiful fossils of jellyfish, moths, and flies. They found fish, crabs, alligators, and *Archaeopteryx*. Because the silt was so fine—almost like powder—the fossils show wonderful details. The lacy wings of dragonflies and the delicate feathers of *Archaeopteryx* are just two examples.

CHAPTER FIVE

A Confusing History

Many people—even scientists—had trouble recognizing fossils of the earliest birds. In 1855, a fossil of some sort of flying animal was discovered in Germany. Scientists decided it came from a pterosaur (TEHR-uh-sawr), one of the flying **reptiles.** Five years later, near the town of Solnhofen, Germany, a fossil feather was found. Although it was only a feather, German

Scientists determined that this fossil belonged to a pterosaur. Similar pterosaur fossils have been found in Africa, Australia, Europe, and North America.

scientist Hermann von Meyer knew it was from an animal that was unknown. He gave it the name *Archaeopteryx*. In 1861, Meyer himself found an *Archaeopteryx* skeleton, again near Solnhofen.

Sixteen years passed before another *Archaeopteryx* was found. This one was a beautiful fossil showing details of the feathers and a mouth full of teeth. In the 1950s, two more skeletons were discovered but were not recognized as birds. Instead, scientists said they were fossils of the little meat-eating dinosaur, *Compsognathus* (KOMP-sog-NATH-us).

In 1970, things began to straighten out. Scientists looked more closely at the little pterosaur skeleton from 1855. They decided it wasn't a flying reptile at all. It was actually the first *Archaeopteryx* ever discovered, but no one had recognized it.

Compsognathus was a small birdlike dinosaur that lived at about the same time as Archaeopteryx.

Later, scientists took a closer look at the two little *Compsognathus* skeletons. As it turned out, they were *Archaeopteryx* fossils as well!

So far, only eight *Archaeopteryx* skeletons have been discovered. These give us a peek into the life of these early birds, but they certainly don't tell us everything. Clearly, there is plenty left to learn.

CHAPTER SIX

GOING BACK IN TIME

O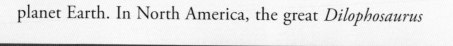ver millions of years, animal life on Earth has changed

a lot. Two hundred million years ago, reptiles ruled

planet Earth. In North America, the great *Dilophosaurus*

Pterosaurs first appeared on Earth about 215 million years ago.

(dih-LO-fuh-sawr-us) and little *Syntarsus* (sin-TAR-sus) hunted

for prey. Plesiosaurs (PLEE-see-o-sawrz) and ichthyosaurs (IK-thee-

o-sawrz) glided through the seas, searching for fish and squid. The

first pterosaurs floated overhead. These were flying reptiles with

leathery wings and tails.

One hundred fifty million years ago, things were very different.

Enormous dinosaurs such as *Diplodocus* (dih-PLOD-uh-kuss) and

Apatosaurus (uh-PAT-uh-SAWR-us) thundered across North America,

searching for bushes and tree branches to eat. Although *Dilophosaurus*

was gone by that time, the big plant eaters still had to watch for other

predators. The fierce *Allosaurus* (AL-o-SAWR-us) could attack at

any time. In Europe, pterosaurs still took to the air, but they were

joined by the first bird—*Archaeopteryx.* Plesiosaurs and ichthyosaurs

still swam the seas.

A variety of animals gathers at an African watering hole.

One hundred million years ago, Earth was different still.

Diplodocus, Apatosaurus, and *Allosaurus* were long gone, replaced

by completely different dinosaurs. *Archaeopteryx* was gone as well.

Fifty million years ago, there were no dinosaurs on Earth.

Every last dinosaur had disappeared about 15 million years earlier.

Not a single plesiosaur or ichthyosaur remained. There were no

pterosaurs in the sky. Instead, snakes, turtles, and lizards were the

main reptiles. The seas were filled with fish and whales. Flying and diving birds were present, as were some large flightless birds.

Mammals ran about on the ground.

Today, more than 7,000 different kinds of reptiles slither,

creep, or skitter across the land, but they are nowhere near the

size of their huge dinosaur

cousins. More than 8,000

kinds of birds exist, but

not a single one has a long,

bony tail like *Archaeopteryx.*

Animal life is constantly

changing. We can only

imagine what the world

will be like in another

50 million years.

Unlike Archaeopteryx, *these king penguins (along with all other modern birds) do not have long, bony tails.*

Glossary

ancestors (AN-sess-turz) Relatives who lived in the past are your ancestors. Because *Archaeopteryx* had so many things in common with the dinosaurs, scientists believe that dinosaurs were the ancestors of birds.

ancient (AYN-shunt) Something that is ancient is very old; from millions of years ago. The name *Archaeopteryx* comes from Greek words meaning "ancient wing."

display (diss-PLAY) A display is a way of showing off. No one knows how the male *Archaeopteryx* courted females, but it probably used some sort of display.

embedded (im-BEH-ded) Something that is embedded is enclosed in, or surrounded by, something else. One *Archaeopteryx*'s body became embedded in the soft mud of a lagoon's floor.

fossils (FOSS-uhlz) Fossils are the things left behind by ancient plants or animals, such as skeletons or footprints. Bird fossils are fairly rare.

lagoon (luh-GOON) A lagoon is a pool that is part of a larger body of water but is still isolated from it. Coral reefs divided the sea into many pools, or lagoons.

predators (PRED-uh-turz) Animals that hunt and eat other animals are predators. Even big, plant-eating dinosaurs had to watch for predators.

prey (PRAY) Animals that are hunted and eaten by others are called prey. *Archaeopteryx* had claws that were curved and may have helped it to catch prey and climb trees.

reptiles (REP-tilez) Reptiles are air-breathing animals with a backbone and are usually covered with scales or plates. Two hundred million years ago, reptiles ruled Earth.

silt (SILT) Silt is very small particles of rock or soil. Fine silt covered the skeletons of fish that died and sank to the bottom of a lagoon.

Did You Know?

▸ Long before scientists realized there were fossils in the Solnhofen Limestone, people were taking its rocks and making them into floor tiles.

▸ Most scientists believe that *Archaeopteryx* could not make long flights.

▸ In 1994, a farmer in China found a bird skeleton that was almost the same age as *Archaeopteryx,* but this bird had no teeth in its beak.

How to Learn More

AT THE LIBRARY

Lambert, David, Darren Naish, and Liz Wyse. *Dinosaur Encyclopedia: From Dinosaurs to the Dawn of Man.* New York: Dorling Kindersley, 2001.

Palmer, Douglas, Barry Cox (editor). *The Simon & Schuster Encyclopedia of Dinosaurs & Prehistoric Creatures: A Visual Who's Who of Prehistoric Life.* New York: Simon & Schuster, 1999.

Schomp, Virginia. *Archaeopteryx and Other Flying Dinosaurs.* New York: Benchmark Books, 2004.

ON THE WEB

Visit our home page for lots of links about *Archaeopteryx*:
http://www.childsworld.com/links.html
NOTE TO PARENTS, TEACHERS, AND LIBRARIANS: We routinely verify our Web links to make sure they're safe, active sites—so encourage your readers to check them out!

PLACES TO VISIT OR CONTACT

AMERICAN MUSEUM OF NATURAL HISTORY
To view numerous dinosaur fossils, as well as the fossils of many ancient mammals
Central Park West at 79th Street
New York, NY 10024-5192
212/769-5100

CARNEGIE MUSEUM OF NATURAL HISTORY
To view a variety of dinosaur skeletons, as well as fossils of other extinct animals
4400 Forbes Avenue
Pittsburgh, PA 15213
412/622-3131

DINOSAUR NATIONAL MONUMENT
To view a huge deposit of dinosaur bones in a natural setting
Dinosaur, CO 81610-9724
or

DINOSAUR NATIONAL MONUMENT (QUARRY)
11625 East 1500 South
Jensen, UT 84035
435/781-7700

MUSEUM OF THE ROCKIES
To see real dinosaur fossils, as well as robotic replicas
Montana State University
600 West Kagy Boulevard
Bozeman, MT 59717-2730
406/994-2251 or 406/994-DINO (3466)

SMITHSONIAN NATIONAL MUSEUM OF NATURAL HISTORY
To see several dinosaur exhibits and take special behind-the-scenes tours
10th Street and Constitution Avenue NW
Washington, DC 20560-0166
202/357-2700

The Geologic Time Scale

CAMBRIAN PERIOD

Date: 540 million to 505 million years ago

Most major animal groups appeared by the end of this period. Trilobites were common and algae became more diversified.

ORDOVICIAN PERIOD

Date: 505 million to 440 million years ago

Marine life became more diversified. Crinoids and blastoids appeared, as did corals and primitive fish. The first land plants appeared. The climate changed greatly during this period—it began as warm and moist, but temperatures ultimately dropped. Huge glaciers formed, causing sea levels to fall.

SILURIAN PERIOD

Date: 440 million to 410 million years ago

Glaciers melted, sea levels rose, and Earth's climate became more stable. Plants with vascular systems developed. This means they had parts that helped them to conduct food and water.

DEVONIAN PERIOD

Date: 410 million to 360 million years ago

Fish became more diverse, as did land plants. The first trees and forests appeared at this time, and the earliest seed-bearing plants began to grow. The first land-living vertebrates and insects appeared. Fossils also reveal evidence of the first ammonoids and amphibians. The climate was warm and mild.

CARBONIFEROUS PERIOD

Date: 360 million to 286 million years ago

The climate was warm and humid, but cooled toward the end of the period. Coal swamps dotted the landscape, as did a multitude of ferns. The earliest reptiles appeared on Earth. Pelycosaurs such as *Edaphosaurus* evolved toward the end of the Carboniferous period.

PERMIAN PERIOD

Date: 286 million to 248 million years ago

Algae, sponges, and corals were common on the ocean floor. Amphibians and reptiles were also prevalent at this time, as were seed-bearing plants and conifers. This period ended with the largest mass extinction on Earth. This may have been caused by volcanic activity or the formation of glaciers and the lowering of sea levels.

TRIASSIC PERIOD

Date: 248 million to 208 million years ago

The climate during this period was warm and dry. The first true mammals appeared, as did frogs, salamanders, and lizards. Evergreen trees made up much of the plant life. The first dinosaurs, including *Coelophysis*, existed on Earth. In the skies, pterosaurs became the earliest winged reptiles to take flight. In the seas, ichthyosaurs and plesiosaurs made their appearance.

JURASSIC PERIOD

Date: 208 million to 144 million years ago

The climate of the Jurassic period was warm and moist. The first birds appeared at this time, and plant life was more diverse and widespread. Although dinosaurs didn't even exist in the beginning of the Triassic period, they ruled Earth by Jurassic times. *Allosaurus, Apatosaurus, Archaeopteryx, Brachiosaurus, Compsognathus, Diplodocus, Ichthyosaurus, Plesiosaurus,* and *Stegosaurus* were just a few of the prehistoric creatures that lived during this period.

CRETACEOUS PERIOD

Date: 144 million to 65 million years ago

The climate of the Cretaceous period was fairly mild. Many modern plants developed, including those with flowers. With flowering plants came a greater diversity of insect life. Birds further developed into two types: flying and flightless. Prehistoric creatures such as *Ankylosaurus, Edmontosaurus, Iguanodon, Maiasaura, Oviraptor, Psittacosaurus, Spinosaurus, Triceratops, Troodon, Tyrannosaurus rex,* and *Velociraptor* all existed during this period. At the end of the Cretaceous period came a great mass extinction that wiped out the dinosaurs, along with many other groups of animals.

TERTIARY PERIOD

Date: 65 million to 1.8 million years ago

Mammals were extremely diversified at this time, and modern-day creatures such as horses, dogs, cats, bears, and whales developed.

QUATERNARY PERIOD

Date: 1.8 million years ago to today

Temperatures continued to drop during this period. Several periods of glacial development led to what is known as the Ice Age. Prehistoric creatures such as glyptodonts, mammoths, mastodons, *Megatherium,* and saber-toothed cats roamed Earth. A mass extinction of these animals occurred approximately 10,000 years ago. The first human beings evolved during the Quaternary period.

Index

About the Author

Susan H. Gray has bachelor's and master's degrees in zoology and has taught college-level courses in biology. She first fell in love with fossil hunting while studying paleontology in college. In her 25 years as an author, she has written many articles for scientists and researchers, and many science books for children. Susan enjoys gardening, traveling, and playing the piano. She and her husband, Michael, live in Cabot, Arkansas.